HAIKU POEMS

By Ruthie Van Oosbree  Poems by Lauren Kukla

Big Buddy Books
An Imprint of Abdo Publishing
abdobooks.com

abdobooks.com

Published by Abdo Publishing, a division of ABDO, PO Box 398166, Minneapolis, Minnesota 55439.

Printed in the United States of America, North Mankato, Minnesota
052022
092022

Design: Emily O'Malley, Mighty Media, Inc.
Production: Mighty Media, Inc.
Editor: Jessica Rusick
Cover Photograph: wavebreakmedia/Shutterstock Images
Interior Photographs: Africa Studio/Shutterstock Images, p. 29; Anneka/Shutterstock Images, p. 6; artshock/Shutterstock Images, p. 25; CHARTGRAPHIC/Shutterstock Images, p. 7; colacat/Shutterstock Images, p. 17; dezy/Shutterstock Images, p. 15 (dog); Joe Gough/Shutterstock Images, p. 20; Konstantin Gushcha/Shutterstock Images, p. 27; Monkey Business Images/Shutterstock Images, p. 11; photomaster/Shutterstock Images, p. 15 (wolf); Quang Ho/Shutterstock Images, p. 13; Rawpixel.com/Shutterstock Images, p. 23; Regreto/Shutterstock Images, p. 18; Ronnie Chua/Shutterstock Images, p. 24; Rostik Solonenko/Shutterstock Images, p. 21; Sean Pavone/Shutterstock Images, p. 5; Sudowoodo/Shutterstock Images, p. 19; Tsekhmister/Shutterstock Images, 12
Design Elements: mhatzapa/Shutterstock Images (paper doodles); Mighty Media, Inc. (backgrounds)

Library of Congress Control Number: 2021953301

Publisher's Cataloging-in-Publication Data
Names: Van Oosbree, Ruthie; Kukla, Lauren, authors.
Title: Haiku poems / by Ruthie Van Oosbree and Lauren Kukla
Description: Minneapolis, Minnesota : Abdo Publishing, 2023 | Series: Poetry power | Includes online resources and index.
Identifiers: ISBN 9781532198946 (lib. bdg.) | ISBN 9781098272876 (ebook)
Subjects: LCSH: Poetry--Juvenile literature. | Poetry and children--Juvenile literature. | Haiku--Juvenile literature. | Rhyme--Juvenile literature.
Classification: DDC 821.0--dc23

CONTENTS

HAIKU

Haiku is a Japanese form of short poetry. It **originated** in the 1200s. Haiku were the first lines of long spoken poems.

In the 1600s, Japanese poets began writing **stand-alone** haiku. The poems often described nature. In the 1900s, haiku became popular around the world.

Japan's cherry blossoms have been a popular haiku subject for centuries.

Japanese poet Matsuo Bashō is considered a haiku master. He was born in 1644. Bashō helped make haiku popular in Japan. His poems are about nature and everyday things. They encourage readers to feel **content**.

An old silent pond . . .

Into the pond a frog jumps,

splash! Silence again.

–Matsuo Bashō

FITTING THE FORM

A haiku has 17 **syllables**. These syllables are divided into three lines of five, seven, and five.

A haiku is usually about a single moment. Many are about nature. Often, haiku describe two different images.

TIPS & TRICKS

Haiku usually reference a season. Try including a word that reflects the season, such as *pumpkin* for fall.

COUNTING SYLLABLES

An old si-lent pond . . .
In-to the pond a frog jumps,
splash! Si-lence a-gain.

● = syllable

NATURE HAIKU

Haiku are often about nature. Go outside and observe the world around you. Watch what happens in each moment.

Try to notice times when two things are together. Maybe a ladybug crawled on a blade of grass. Maybe the wind blew a leaf into a puddle.

Take a nature walk for inspiration!

Write about a moment that made you feel **content**. Or choose an unusual or interesting image. Cut your words down to create your haiku.

The spring flower blooms,
inviting the honeybee
to stay for a while.

ANIMAL HAIKU

Animals are great haiku subjects. They often act in fun and interesting ways.

Write about a pet. Think about your pet's favorite activities. Or, write about a wild animal. Where does it live? How does it act?

TIPS & TRICKS

Many haiku contain two images that don't usually go together. Try to write about an unexpected pair of images, like a little dog and a wolf!

My little dog runs,

darting through wild autumn woods,

a wolf inside her.

HUMOROUS HAIKU

Many poets write **humorous** haiku. Your haiku could be about something silly a friend did. It could be about a funny moment you saw on TV. Or it could be about something funny that happened to you!

Your poem could
be about a goofy
animal!

Gross things can be funny too. Write about an icky smell or a weird noise. Try to make the last line of your haiku unexpected. It can be like the **punch line** of a joke!

Something smells quite bad,
like old cheese or stinky feet.
Time to clean my room.

FOOD HAIKU

People use their senses when they eat. They see, smell, taste, and touch their food. They might even hear it **sizzling**.

Use your senses to write a food haiku. You might write about a favorite food. Or write about a gross food!

On a cold morning,
the smell of bacon frying
is the best alarm.

SPORTS HAIKU

Sports are full of action. This can make for exciting haiku! A haiku can show a fun, difficult, or **dramatic** sports moment.

What is your favorite sport? You could write about a game you attended or saw on TV. Or write about a game you played in.

Try writing about a coach who inspires you!

Think about a short but important moment from the game. It could be as simple as a ball hitting a bat. Maybe there was a great pass or catch. Break the moment down into small details. Use these details in your haiku.

I fly on the ice
skating to the puck, stick raised.
Then I shoot and SCORE!

FAVORITE THINGS HAIKU

Use haiku to show your love for a favorite object. This could be a stuffed animal or toy. Or your object could have to do with a hobby.

Think about your object. What do you like about it? How does it make you feel? Write your haiku using these details.

Your tattered whiskers
will never overshadow
your bright loving eyes.

SHARING YOUR HAIKU

Haiku were originally spoken aloud. Follow this **tradition** to share your haiku! Read your poem to friends, family, or classmates.

Some ancient haiku had **illustrations**. Draw a picture to go with your haiku. Then hang your poem up!

Write your haiku
in color to make
it pop.

GLOSSARY

content (kuhn-TENT)—happy, peaceful, and satisfied.

dramatic—exciting or emotional.

humorous—funny or amusing.

illustration—a picture or drawing.

originate—to create or begin.

punch line—the sentence or phrase at the end of a joke that makes the joke funny.

sizzle—to make a hissing sound when cooking.

stand-alone—complete on its own.

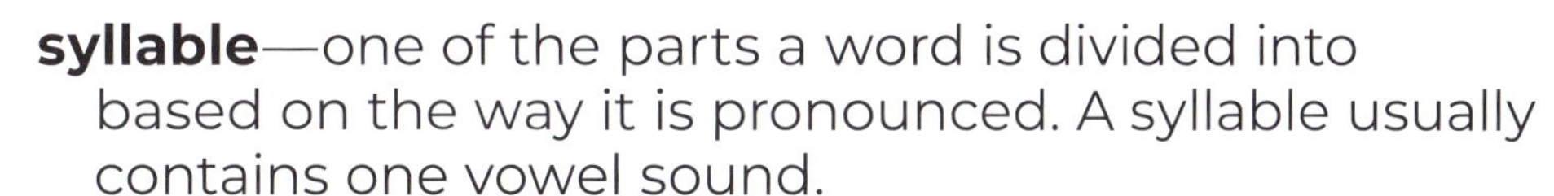

syllable—one of the parts a word is divided into based on the way it is pronounced. A syllable usually contains one vowel sound.

tradition (truh-DIH-shuhn)—a belief, custom, or story handed down from older people to younger people.

ONLINE RESOURCES

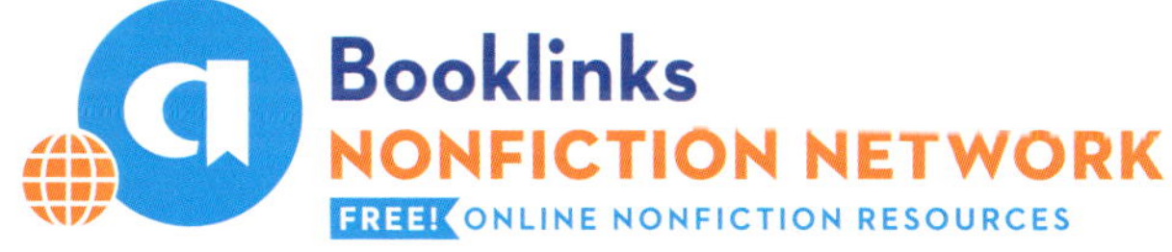

To learn more about haiku poems, please visit **abdobooklinks.com** or scan this QR code. These links are routinely monitored and updated to provide the most current information available.

INDEX